Kid's Library of Space Exploration

Deep-Space Probes

Kid's Library of Space Exploration

Kid's Library of Space Exploration

Deep-Space Probes

Kim Etingoff

Kid's Library of Space Exploration:
Deep-Space Probes

Village Earth Press
Vestal, New York 13850
www.villageearthpress.com

First Printing
9 8 7 6 5 4 3 2 1

Series ISBN (paperback): 978-1-62524-444-4
ISBN (paperback): 978-1-62524-406-2
ebook ISBN: 978-1-62524-041-5
    Library of Congress Control Number: 2014931526

Author: Etingoff, Kim.

Contents

ONE

Early History

For as long as humans have existed, we have looked out into the night sky and wondered what was up there. Stars, planets, the Milky Way—they have all fascinated us, even before we knew what they were.

With today's science, we can explore all those wonders. We can put satellites in orbit around the Earth. We have sent people to the moon. We're even sending spacecraft out beyond the solar system.

What Is Deep Space?

Scientists have done a pretty good job of exploring what's near Earth. We know a lot about outer space just outside the Earth's *atmosphere*. We've learned a lot about the Earth. In the

The **atmosphere** is the layer of gases that surrounds the Earth. Most planets have atmospheres, but, as far as we know, we can only breathe in the Earth's.

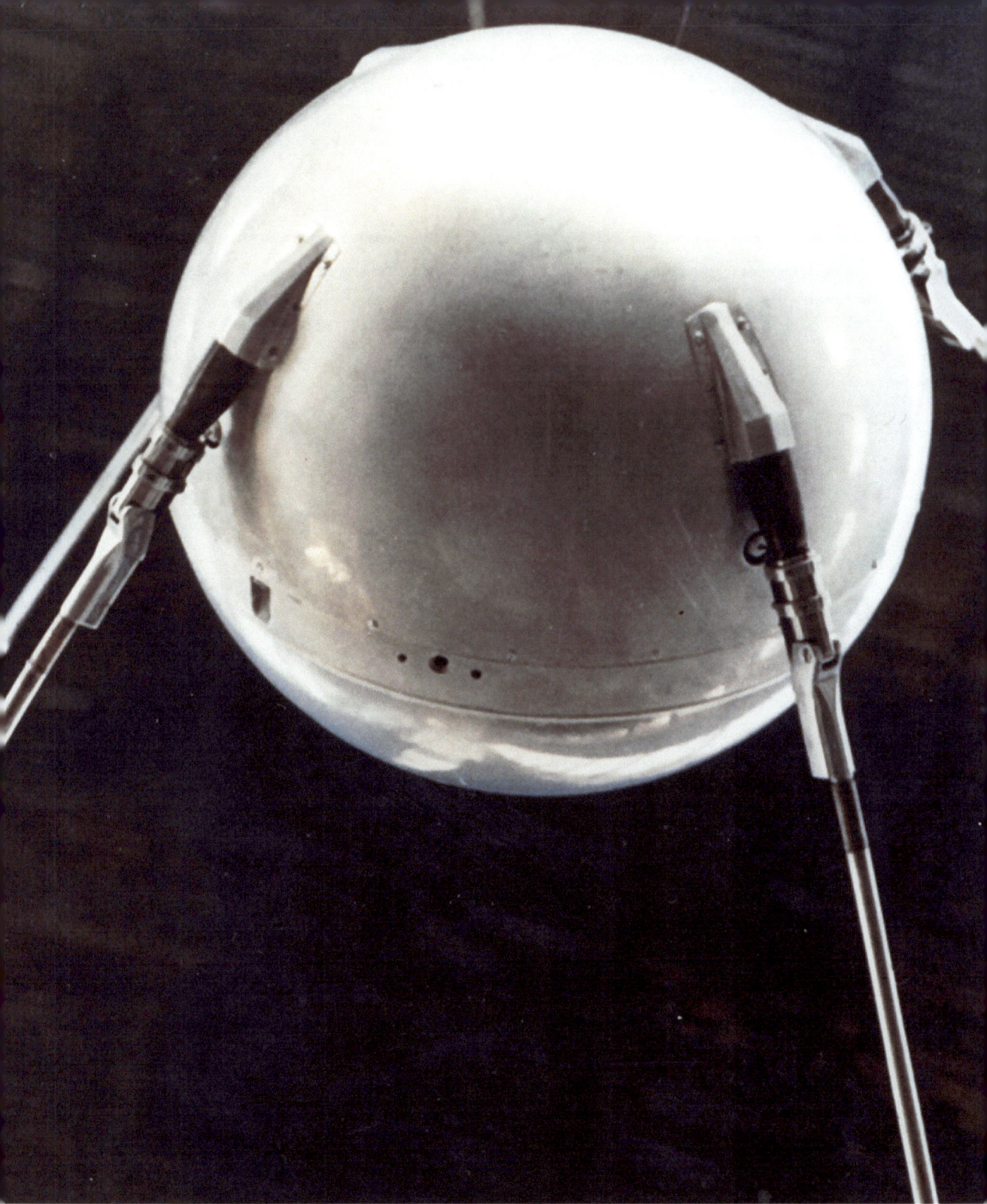

Sputnik 1 was the first probe ever launched into orbit. It didn't go very far, but it taught scientists a lot about how to get objects into space.

twenty-first century, spacecraft are giving us all sorts of new information about Mars, one of our nearest neighbors.

But we don't know a lot about "deep space." Deep space is everywhere that is distant from Earth. Scientists think of parts of our solar system as deep space, like Jupiter, Saturn, and beyond. Deep space is also outside our solar system. Space is huge! Most of space is "deep space" to us.

We don't know a lot about deep space because it takes a long time to get there. People can get to the moon in a few days. Getting past the solar system takes years and years. People have also been busy exploring other parts of space, like the moon and Mars. We haven't had time or money yet to really focus on deep space.

Some of that is changing, though. A few spacecraft have made it out very far into space. We're learning more every day.

Our space exploration really started in the 1950s. The technology and knowledge we had then led to where we are now. Sending anything into space back then was a big achievement!

First Satellites

A satellite is any human-made object that circles a planet or moon. Right now, the Earth has thousands of satellites circling it.

Back in the 1950s, there weren't any satellites. No one had ever sent anything up into space before. Then, in 1957, someone did.

The Soviet Union (which is now Russia and several other countries) sent the first satellite into space on October 4, 1957. The satellite was called *Sputnik 1*. This first satellite was pretty tiny. *Sputnik 1* was about as big as a beach ball. It weighed just under 200 pounds (about 90 kilograms). One orbit around the Earth took about an hour and a half.

A month later, the Soviet Union launched *Sputnik 2*. This *Sputnik* was bigger. It also carried a live dog named Laika.

On the other side of the world, the American government was angry and jealous. The United States had wanted to be the first country in the world to launch a satellite. The Soviets had beaten the United States to it.

During the 1950s, the United States and the Soviet Union were competing. Both wanted to be the most powerful country in the world. They

Above, William Pickering, James Van Allen, and Wernher von Braun hold a model of Explorer 1. *The radiation belt that* Explorer *discovered is named the Van Allen belt, after the scientist who helped find it.*

were building up weapons. They were convincing different countries to take their side.

Now they were competing to see who could be the best in space. As soon as the Soviet Union sent up *Sputnik 1* and *2*, the space race was on. Each country tried to get to the next step in space exploration first.

At first, the United States didn't have much luck. They tried to launch a satellite, but the rocket it was on exploded during liftoff.

Then, in 1958, the United States sent up its own satellite. The United States launched *Explorer 1*. The satellite was longer and skinnier than *Sputnik*. It took two hours to orbit the Earth.

Although *Explorer* wasn't the first satellite in space, it still sent back lots of useful information. For example, the satellite discovered belts of *radiation* around the planet. It was an important discovery because astronauts would need to be protected from the radiation when they went into space. We also learned that the Earth's atmosphere and magnetic field protect us from most of the radiation, which is why it doesn't usually hurt us.

Later on, the United States sent up more *Explorer* satellites. Some of them made it to space. Some of them didn't. Scientists were still learning.

At the start of the space race, the American government created the National Aeronautics and Space Administration (NASA). NASA would be in charge of space exploration. NASA is still working today, leading space exploration in the United States.

The Race to the Moon

In 1961, U.S. President John F. Kennedy promised that the United States would land a person on the moon by the end of the 1960s. NASA then launched the *Apollo* program. They designed a spacecraft to bring people to the moon and back to Earth. Several *Apollo* spacecraft sent people by and around the moon. *Apollo 11* was the first mission to actually land people on the moon. Astronauts Neil Armstrong, Buzz Aldrin, and Michael Collins made history on July 20, 1969. The United States had won the space race.

Radiation is dangerous energy that can be harmful to humans. There's lots of radiation in space, but our atmosphere usually protects us.

Pioneer 1, *shown here, was meant to go to the moon. It didn't make it all the way there, but it did transmit 43 hours of information back to NASA.*

Pioneers

Both the United States and the Soviet Union were leaders in space exploration. As the space race heated up, the two countries competed to see who could get a human on the moon first. The United States succeeded in 1969.

But other things were going on too. NASA had other missions besides those that were going to the moon.

NASA also had the *Pioneer* program. The *Pioneer* missions were space probes. They were sent out into space to gather lots of new information. Each one had a slightly different goal and destination.

The first few *Pioneer* space probes didn't do very well. Some didn't even make it into space.

The later *Pioneer* missions were much more successful. They were sent out to explore interplanetary space—the space between planets in our solar system.

Pioneer 6, 7, 8, and *9* were space probes that orbited the Sun. They had lots of instruments to measure *data* in space. They measured *solar* radiation. They measured solar wind. They measured the sun's *magnetic field*. Scientists learned a lot about the sun and the space between the Earth and the sun.

Although they sent back a lot of new information, each *Pioneer* spacecraft was small. They were cone shaped, three feet across, and three feet high (about one meter across and one meter high).

The tiny satellites lasted a long time. NASA designed them

Jupiter's Great Red Spot

Jupiter is a huge planet. And on Jupiter is a huge storm we can even see through a telescope from Earth. The storm is always there. It's called the Great Red Spot on Jupiter. That storm is big enough to fit three Earth's into it! However, the Great Red Spot is shrinking and may one day disappear. Scientists don't know much about what exactly causes the storm, or what keeps it going. They hope to learn more.

Data is scientific information that is gathered during an experiment.

Solar has to do with the sun.

Every planet and star has a **magnetic field**. This field has a north and a south, like a giant version of a regular magnet.

Jupiter's Great Red Spot is so huge that we can see it from Earth—but this was one of the first close looks scientists got of it, when Voyager 1 *passed by Jupiter in 1979.*

to last six months in space. All four actually lasted a lot longer. Scientists last heard from *Pioneer* 6 in 2000. It wasn't being used anymore, but thirty-five years after its launch, NASA contacted *Pioneer* 6, just to see if they could—and they did!

Pioneer 10 and 11

NASA was ready for something more complicated. *Pioneer 10* was launched in 1972. Its mission was to fly to Jupiter.

Pioneer 10 was the fastest man-made object to leave Earth in history. It rocketed away at 32,400 miles per hour (52,100 kilometers per hour).

First, it passed by the moon and Mars. Then the space probe made its way through the asteroid belt, an area full of dust and rocks hurtling through space. Finally, *Pioneer 10* arrived at Jupiter.

Pioneer 10 took the first close photos of Jupiter people had ever seen. Astronomers had only been able to look at it through telescopes until then. The space probe also measured Jupiter's radiation and magnetic fields.

Its journey wasn't over yet. *Pioneer 10* flew past Jupiter into the rest of the solar system. In fact, it kept sending back information about the solar system until 1997! Even after that, NASA could sometimes communicate with it years later.

A year after *Pioneer 10*, NASA sent up *Pioneer 11*. Like *Pioneer 10*, this one was sent to the outer solar system. *Pioneer 11* flew by Jupiter. But its main goal was Saturn, the next planet out.

Pioneer 11 got more close-up photos of Jupiter, including the Great Red Spot. Then, when it reached Saturn, the probe also took beautiful photos. It discovered two moons and another of Saturn's rings. It also took lots of measurements. Now scientists had a lot more information about Saturn.

And *Pioneer 11* kept going. Its instruments measured solar wind (particles of energy that come from the sun) and other things. By the

Pioneer's Instruments

Here's a list of all the instruments onboard *Pioneer 11*. Each one measured something different. They all helped scientists learn more about our solar system.

asteroid-meteoroid
   experiment
charged particle instrument
   cosmic ray telescope
flux-gate magnetometer
Geiger tube telescope
helium vector
   magnetometer
imaging photopolarimeter
infrared radiometer
meteoroid detector
plasma analyzer
trapped radiation detector
ultraviolet photometer

```
NASA ARC                    PIONEER 10          UNIV ARIZ
RANGE:    2965000 KM    PHASE:    28.7    LCM2:    20
DATA RECEIVED 1 DEC 22:17:08 TO 1 DEC 22:37:46
A58 COLOR SECTOR 154 - 441   B  06/11/74
```

Pioneer 10 took this picture of Jupiter as it flew by in 1975. Since this picture was taken, the Great Red Spot has shrunk by about 10,000 miles (25,000 km)—about 40% of its size.

time *Pioneer 11* stopped communicating with NASA, it was 6.5 billion miles (10.5 billion kilometers or 70 *astronomical units*) away.

Both probes also had something beside instruments onboard. They had golden plaques that were meant to communicate to any living thing that might find them somewhere in space. The plaques had pictures of a woman and a man on them. If anyone finds the plaque, they'll know what humans look like. Other symbols show how far the Earth is from the Sun, and a picture of the solar system. Hopefully, someday, someone—or something!—will be able to decode it.

By now, both *Pioneer* space probes have left the solar system. They were the first man-made objects to do so. Unless they crash into something, they'll keep speeding away for a very long time. In 2 million years, *Pioneer 10* is on track to pass by the star Aldebaran, which is part of the Taurus constellation, a long, long way from Earth.

Two more *Pioneers* were later launched to study Venus. *Pioneer 12* reached Venus successfully and started mapping out what it could "see." Scientists now have a good idea of what Venus's atmosphere, clouds, and surface look like. After fourteen years in orbit, *Pioneer 12* crashed into Venus's atmosphere.

Pioneer 13 also went to Venus. The other *Pioneers* had only been one probe each. *Pioneer 13* was actually four probes! A larger spacecraft transported all four probes to Venus, and then let them go.

The *Pioneer* missions were our first real attempts at exploring deep space. And they were successful! Scientists were learning all sorts of new things about what lies beyond Earth.

Life on Mars

When we talk about finding life on other planets, we're usually not talking about big, complicated life forms like plants, animals, and people. It's much more likely that we'll find microscopic forms of life, like bacteria or other kinds of germs. This would still be pretty exciting, though—so far, Earth is the only planet where we're completely sure that any kind of life can exist.

An **astronomical unit** is the distance between Earth and the sun—about 93 million miles (150 million km)!

The Viking 1 *spacecraft launches from Cape Canaveral, in Florida.*

DEEP-SPACE PROBES

The Viking *missions took some of the first pictures of the Martian surface. The circle at the top of the image is the lander's antenna, pointing home to Earth.*

Pathfinder

While the *Pioneer* probes were busy exploring Jupiter, Saturn, and Venus, a different spacecraft was exploring Mars.

For several years in the 1960s and 1970s, scientists from the United States and Soviet Union had been sending probes to fly around Mars. The probes were called Mars orbiters. The orbiters took pictures of the surface and made some measurements.

In 1975, two orbiters from the United States landed safely on Mars. They were *Viking 1* and *Viking 2*. The *Viking* missions were the first major explorations of Mars. We found the first evidence that there might be water on Mars.

Then NASA sent the *Pathfinder* mission to Mars. *Pathfinder* was a Mars lander, meaning it was a spacecraft that landed on the surface.

Engineers have come up with many ways to get spacecraft safely to the surface of Mars. These large airbags are designed to protect the Pathfinder spacecraft as they fall to the ground.

Inside was a rover called *Sojourner*. The rover could actually move around the surface and collect samples of rocks and soil to do experiments on.

The lander successfully flew to Mars. Then it entered the Martian atmosphere. Rockets and a parachute slowed it down, so it wouldn't crash into the surface. Then it bounced around on the surface on air bags. Finally, it came to rest.

Pathfinder was ready to release its rover. The door opened, and *Sojourner* came out. The rover had six wheels and a solar panel on its flat back. It was small, but it could do a lot!

Together, *Pathfinder* and *Sojourner* took lots of pictures and did some experiments. They sent back useful information. Most importantly, they proved that scientists could do this kind of mission again.

Pathfinder was the most complicated mission sent into deep space yet. Even more advanced rovers were sent later, but this was the first.

Maybe someday we will send landers and rovers to other planets deeper in space. We could be exploring the rest of the planets someday.

Find Out Even More

Books like the one you're reading now can hold a lot of information. Reading books is a great way to learn about amazing subjects like space probes. But one book can never tell you everything about a subject.

Authors find facts and stories about their subjects. They organize the information in a way you can easily understand. But authors have to choose what to leave out. To get more information, you have to read more than one book. Books are a great way to learn more about any topic you love. But no one book is perfect.

To find other books about the subjects you're interested in, head to a library near you. Your school may have a library. If not, you can probably find a local library nearby. At the library, you can find new books in the library's card catalog. You can also find new books by asking the librarian. The books listed below might be a good list to get started with. If the library near you doesn't have these books, you can probably find other books about space exploration and space probes.

Kortenkamp, Steve. *Space Probes (First Facts)*. North Mankato, Minn.: Capstone, 2007.

Goldsmith, Mike. *Universe: Journey Into Deep Space*. New York: Kingfisher, 2012.

Kerrod, Robin and Chris Woodford. *Space Probes (History of Space Exploration)*. New York: Gareth Stevens Publishing, 2004.

Stott, Carole. *Space Exploration*. New York: DK Publishing, 2009.

Take a close look inside one of the books you find in the library. Check out the table of contents. Flip to a chapter that you're curious about. Take a look at some of the chapter's pages. Read a page or two. Leaf over a few more pages in the book and then ask yourself a few questions:

1. How well do you understand the book? Each reader is different just as each book is different. Becoming a better reader is about finding books that you can understand. But don't forget to challenge yourself a bit!
2. How is the book organized? Does the book have a glossary? Does it have an index? Is it easy to find information by using the index and table of contents?
3. Looking at the table of contents and index, are there subjects in this book you haven't read in other books about space probes?
4. Are there pictures or photos in the book? Do they help to understand the subject of the book? Check out the captions (words under the photos or illustrations). How do they help you understand the picture?

TWO

The First True Probes

The *Pioneer* probes have gone pretty far out in space. But they weren't designed to keep sending back information all the way out there.

For that, scientists needed new spacecraft. NASA came up with the *Voyager* program. Two *Voyagers* were sent out to deep space, past the outer planets and beyond.

Jupiter and Saturn

NASA decided to build two identical deep-space explorers. They launched both of them in 1977. *Voyager 2* was launched in August, and *Voyager 1* was launched in September. NASA picked 1977 because of the way the planets were lined up. The spacecraft could sligshot around each one for a boost of speed, and they wouldn't need to carry as much fuel.

The first mission for the *Voyagers* was to study Jupiter and Saturn. Scientists wanted to learn more about these planets.

The Voyager 2 spacecraft sits on the launch pad in 1977. The two Voyager spacecraft are still in operation—after "slingshotting" by the outer planets in the solar system, they flew into interstellar space, where they're still sending back data.

Each probe carried lots of instruments to do experiments. There were cameras to take pictures too. The probes are nuclear powered. Most spacecraft have solar panels and are powered by the sun. The *Voyagers* were traveling too far away from the sun to use solar panels, though, so they used a special kind of battery. As the materials inside the battery broke down, they would release energy to power the spacecraft. These nuclear batteries wouldn't run out of power for a long time, though—they could last for almost a hundred years!

NASA had built *Voyager 1* and *2* to last for five years. Scientists figured that five years would be enough to get lots of information about Jupiter and Saturn.

Voyager 1 made it to Jupiter in 1979. *Voyager 2* got there a few months later. They took pictures of the storms on Jupiter. They found that Jupiter has a faint ring of rocks around it, like Saturn has rings.

Deep Space Network

A system called the Deep Space Network (DSN) lets people on Earth communicate with spacecraft that are very far away in deep space. Around the world, the network has antennas, computers, and other technology that pick up the signals the spacecraft send. The DSN has three sites where most of the technology lives—one in the state of California, one in Australia, and one in Madrid, Spain. The two *Voyager* missions are still sending signals back through the DSN today.

The probes also explored Jupiter's moons. They discovered that Io, one of the moons, has several active volcanoes. And they discovered entirely new moons too. The *Voyagers* sent back data on Jupiter's magnetic field, atmosphere, and more.

Then *Voyager 1* traveled on to Saturn in 1980. *Voyager 2* made it in 1981. They made some new discoveries about Saturn, especially its rings. They found that Saturn's rings were probably made from moons that had been broken apart by meteoroids. All the rock that had been blown apart was caught by Saturn's gravity, and starting spinning around the planet in a ring.

After the Jupiter and Saturn explorations, both *Voyagers* had done their jobs. They did what scientists had built them to do. Now what?

Meteoroids are chunks of rock and metal flying through space.

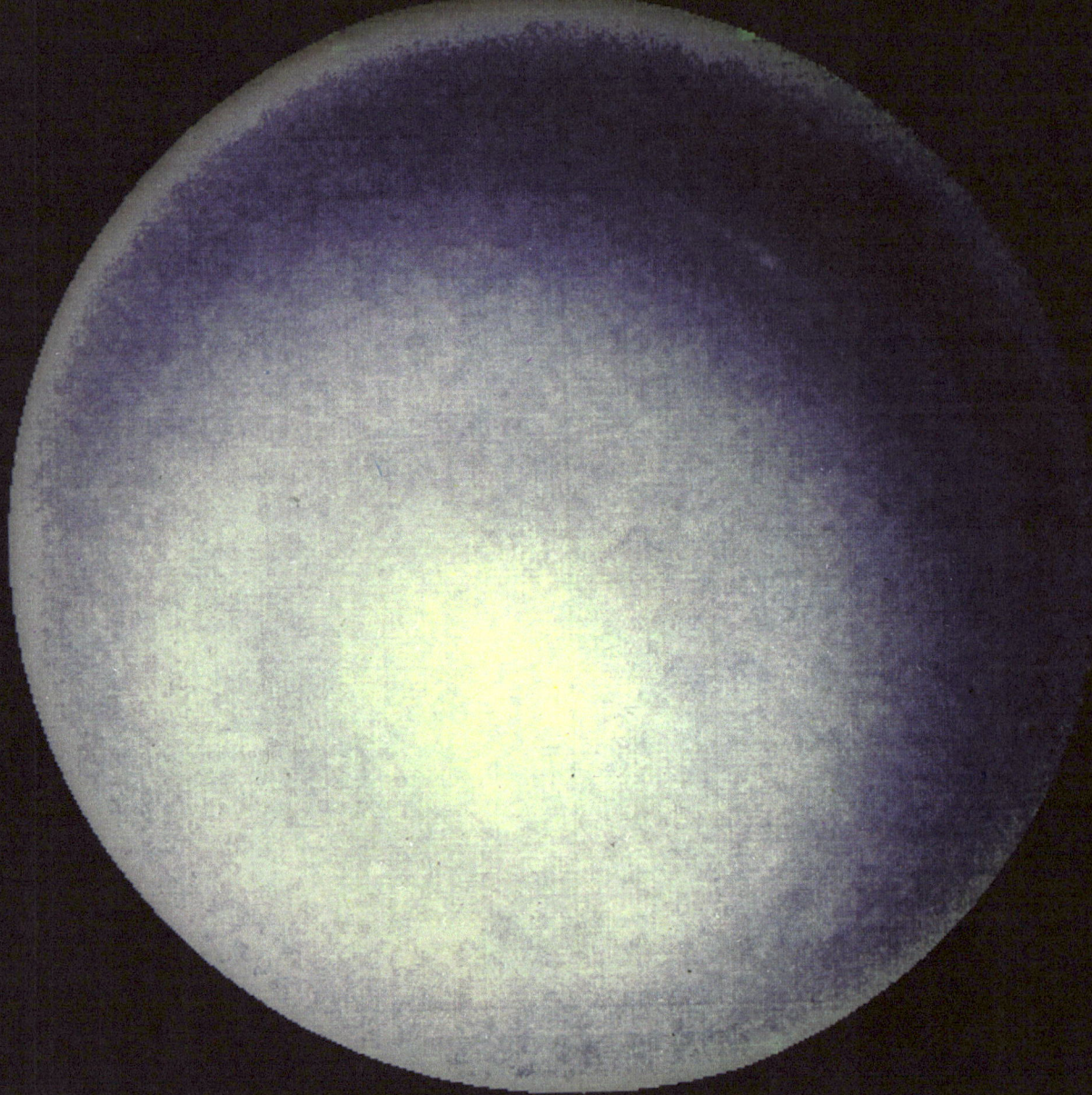

Uranus is probably covered with the same kinds of storms we can see on Jupiter and Saturn—but thick haze in the upper atmosphere hides the details.

Uranus and Neptune

NASA had always thought about sending space probes to Uranus and Neptune, the outermost planets in our solar system. But scientists thought it would be too hard and too expensive.

Luckily, the *Voyager* probes could do the job. After they had flown by Jupiter and Saturn, they were both working fine.

Voyager 2 was on track to fly by Uranus and Neptune. NASA had planned it that way just in case the space probe was still working by the time it was done exploring Jupiter and Saturn. So *Voyager 2* kept going. It was the first (and so far, only) spacecraft to make it to Uranus. Scientists didn't really know what to expect, because no one had ever explored the planet.

Voyager 2 made lots of discoveries, just like it had with Jupiter and Saturn. Uranus has a tilted magnetic field, because the planet itself is tilted. The poles don't sit north and south like on Earth. Instead, they are diagonal (kitty-corner) from each other, probably because something big crashed into Uranus a long time ago.

The space probe also discovered ten new moons. It measured the temperature at the surface at –350 degrees Fahrenheit (–212 degrees Celsius)! And it explored Uranus's rings.

Moons

Some of the biggest discoveries *Voyager 1* and *2* made were moons. The two space probes discovered moons on every planet they explored—twenty-two in all. Many of those moons are really amazing. On Mimas, one of Saturn's moons, pictures showed a huge crater. The crater was so big that the meteoroid that caused it must have almost broken apart the whole moon. One of Neptune's moons, called Triton, has a lot of interesting things going on. Geysers rocket dust and gas up into the air. Triton actually orbits Neptune in the opposite direction from which Neptune spins. Its orbit is called a retrograde orbit.

Next, it was on to Neptune. People didn't know much about Neptune either. *Voyager 2* would teach them a lot about the farthest planet in the solar system.

Neptune is really far away. The planet is so far from the Sun that it takes 165 years for it to make one circle around it.

Voyager 2 found six new moons around Neptune. It measured Neptune's day, and it found big storms on the surface of the planet. The storms were a lot like the Great Red Spot on Jupiter.

Instruments on board measured the temperature, the wind, radiation, and the magnetic field. Now scientists knew almost as much about Neptune as they did about other planets in deep space.

Voyager 2's pictures of Neptune showed the storms and cloud formations seen here. Years later, when Hubble looked at Neptune, these features had disappeared or changed.

Beyond

NASA wasn't done with the *Voyager* spacecraft. They had been flying for twelve years, but they had more to do. Now they had a new mission: the Voyager Interstellar Mission (VIM). The goal of the VIM is to explore the outer limits of the solar system. Before *Voyager*, people had never been able to get data from a spacecraft out there.

Many of the instruments the *Voyagers* are carrying still work. Some have been turned off to save power. But many still collect information and send it all the way back to Earth!

After exploring Saturn for a while, *Voyage 1* went off farther into deep space. *Voyager 2* first went to Uranus and Neptune. Then it traveled off into deep space in a different direction from *Voyager 1*.

For several years, the *Voyager* missions were in the first part of the VIM. They were still within reach of the Sun's magnetic field. There was still a lot of solar wind.

Then they each hit interstellar wind (from space beyond the reach of the Sun). The solar wind the probes were flying through was slower now.

Right now, both *Voyagers* are passing through the last places where they can feel the Sun's magnetic field and solar wind. The area is called the heliopause. Once they're outside of that, they will have crossed out of the solar system. Who knows what they will find next!

Find Out Even More

Reading is one of the best ways to find more information about probes in deep space. But books can only cover so much. They aren't always the best source of information. And they aren't the only source either. Using the Internet is another great way to look up information about subjects you love. Online, there is no limit to the information you can find.

Books are great because the author does the work for you. Each author brings you the facts and stories that he finds the most interesting. But that means some facts don't make it in. On the Internet, you have to find the facts yourself. You can read other people's ideas and take on the facts online too, of course. But you can also find out a lot of information on your own. It may be more work, but you can do it if you're curious!

One of best ways to find information online is using search engines. Search engines like Google and Bing help give you the sites that will be closest to what you want. But search engines find sites based on what you type into the search bar. These words are called key words. Key words are short groups of words that help to give the search engine an idea of what kind of results you want. Try searching for some of the key words below.

National Aeronautics and Space Administration (NASA)
Sputnik
Voyager

European Space Agency (ESA)
Mars
Explorer
Apollo
Deep Space Network
Great Red Spot
Italian Space Agency
Pathfinder
Sojourner

Search engines like Google and Bing can only find sites based on what key words you use, so picking the right words is important. Learning more about any subject is easy on the Internet. But the wrong search words can bring you search results that aren't even close to what you want. Want to know more about the ESA? Make sure you don't end up at the Eastern Surfing Association's website!

THREE

Exploring Our Own Solar System

Voyager 1 and 2 were heading out into deep space beyond the solar system. But the solar system itself was still a mystery to scientists. Even today, we only know a little bit of what there is to know about the solar system.

To learn more, NASA sent out two space probes to deep space within the solar system. *Galileo* was sent to explore Jupiter. *Cassini* was sent to explore Saturn.

Galileo

After the *Voyager* flybys of Jupiter and Saturn, NASA wanted to know more. We were learning a lot about the moon, Mars, and other

Unlike other probes, Galileo *was not launched on its own rocket. Instead, the space shuttle* Atlantis *carried it into orbit and launched it from there.*

close-by space objects. But what about planets and moons deeper in space?

NASA launched the *Galileo* space probe in 1989. It was going to go to Jupiter, to build on what the *Voyagers* had shown us. The spacecraft was named after the famous astronomer Galileo Galilei. In the sixteenth century, Galileo made many discoveries about the night sky. NASA was hoping their space probe would do the same.

Galileo was sent up in the space shuttle *Atlantis* in October 1989. It weighed six thousand pounds (2700 kg) and was about twenty feet (six meters) tall. After astronaut Shannon Lucid let it go from the shuttle, it traveled through the solar system. Six years later, *Galileo* would reach Jupiter. But first, the spacecraft had to get enough power to get all the way to Jupiter. It used the gravity from Venus and Earth to fling itself out into space, kind of like a slingshot.

NASA had a chance to try out *Galileo*'s instruments on its way to Jupiter. When it flew by Earth, the antenna didn't open right, though. Scientists figured out a way to use a different antenna instead. Space exploration can be hard! Scientists have to be creative and fix last-minute problems.

Even before *Galileo* got to Jupiter, it sent back some pretty amazing pictures. It took a close-up look at Venus. It traveled through the asteroid belt and took the first detailed pictures of an asteroid ever.

Finally, the spacecraft got close to Jupiter. It let go of the smaller space probe inside. The probe floated down through Jupiter's atmosphere, sending back weather measurements.

The weather on Jupiter isn't like the weather on Earth! The planet has winds that measured 300 to 400 miles an hour (480 to 640 kilometers per hour). There weren't many clouds. It was very hot.

After less than an hour, the probe melted. Jupiter was too hot. Scientists had known that would happen, though, and they were prepared. The rest of the spacecraft kept orbiting above Jupiter. It orbited eleven times over two years.

One of the big things *Galileo* explored was Jupiter's magnetosphere—its magnetic field. The magnetometer on board measures the magnetic field.

Galileo was still going strong after two years. NASA decided the spacecraft would next study two of Jupiter's moons, along with Jupiter's huge storms.

When testing spacecraft, scientists have to try to simulate the conditions they will experience on other planets. Here, the Galileo *lander's parachute system is tested in a wind tunnel.*

The spacecraft flew very close by the moon Europa. Europa is covered in ice, but *Galileo* observed that it might also have an ocean of liquid water underneath that ice. Liquid water would be an exciting discovery—it might mean life in another part of the solar system. *Galileo* also flew by the moon Io. It saw volcanoes erupting on Io.

Jupiter has a lot of radiation. We experience radiation here on Earth, from the Sun. That's why we wear sunblock when we go outside. On Jupiter, the radiation is a lot higher. Over time, the radiation from Jupiter was wearing down *Galileo*.

In 2004, scientists crashed *Galileo* into Jupiter. It burned up. Scientists were glad for the many years *Galileo* had explored Jupiter and its moons. They know new even more about this planet in deep space.

Cassini

After *Galileo*, NASA wanted to explore Saturn too. While *Galileo* was exploring Jupiter, NASA was building a new space probe called *Cassini*. This one would travel to Saturn.

NASA launched the *Cassini* spacecraft in October 1997. Inside was the *Huygens* probe. The European Space Agency (ESA) designed the probe. The ESA is like NASA in Europe. The Italian Space Agency (Agenzia Spaziale Italiana) also worked with the two other organizations.

Cassini is a lot bigger than *Galileo*. It weighs 12,600 pounds (5700 kg)! It has three antennas, one of which helps protect it from the Sun's rays.

Cassini has lots of instruments to take measurements and do experiments. It has instruments to measure ultraviolet radiation and infrared rays. These are special types of light that humans can't see with their eyes. Cassini can also measure Saturn's magnetosphere. It has regular cameras on board, too!

The spacecraft reached Saturn in 2004. Flying to Saturn had taken seven years, since Saturn is so far away. *Cassini* traveled 2.2 billion miles (3.5 billion kilometers or 24 astronomical units) to get to Saturn.

Cassini and *Huygens* together had eighteen instruments on board to do experiments. Together, they had a lot of questions to answer. Scientists wanted to know where Saturn's rings came from, and why they were different colors. They wanted to see if there were any more moons

Although Cassini *would swing by Earth and Venus to work up speed, its real mission was to study Saturn. It was supposed to orbit Saturn for four years, but it's still going!*

orbiting Saturn. They wanted to figure out why the planet produced heat.

A lot of the exciting things the spacecraft found had to do with Saturn's moons. *Cassini* ended up discovering three more moons. It even found evidence of liquid water on one of them, the moon called Enceladus. *Cassini* found landslides on another, and a big lake of methane on another. Methane is an organic molecule that we have here on Earth. It might mean that life could form on that moon!

The *Huygens* probe was sent down to the surface of one of Saturn's moons, called Titan. People already knew Titan was very interesting. It has the gas methane. It also has nitrogen, another kind of gas that we have in our atmosphere here on Earth. Titan is a lot more like Earth than most other things in the solar system. Maybe it even has life. *Huygens* was going to help scientists figure it out.

What Is a Magnetosphere?

A magnetosphere is the area around a planet that is magnetized by that planet. When you play with a magnet, you can see how strong its magnetic field is by testing how close it has to get to iron objects before it pulls them toward itself. That's kind of like a planet's magnetosphere. Earth has one. So do Jupiter and the other planets. Jupiter's magnetosphere is really big and really powerful. Instruments on *Galileo* measured how strong the magnetosphere is, and what it does to the planet, moons, and solar wind coming from the Sun.

Huygens traveled down through Titan's atmosphere for two and a half hours. The probe eventually landed on the surface. While on Titan, *Huygens* took pictures. It measured the gases in the atmosphere and how fast the wind was. Scientists now had a lot more information about Titan.

Huygens' mission was done now, since it couldn't get off the surface of Titan, but *Cassini* was still going strong. Like a lot of other spacecraft, *Cassini* has lasted a lot longer than it was built to last. It reached the end of its planned mission in 2008. But it was still working just fine.

So NASA gave *Cassini* a new mission—the *Cassini* Equinox Mission. For two more years, the spacecraft flew by some of Saturn's moons several times. It especially focused on Titan.

Building the Cassini *probe* was a huge job. The finished probe was two stories high, and is the largest interplanetary spacecraft ever built!

Even then, *Cassini* was still going, so NASA gave it a third mission, called the *Cassini* Solstice Mission. That mission is supposed to keep going until 2017. If it works until then, *Cassini* will have been flying around Saturn for twenty years. That's a long time to study one planet. And even then, we might get a fourth mission out of the long-lasting spacecraft!

Mission Cost

Space exploration is really expensive! The *Cassini* mission cost $1.422 billion before it was even launched. In all, including the flight itself, the mission has cost over $3 billion. NASA paid for most of it, while the ESA paid for about $700 million. And that's just one mission—NASA has lots and lots more space exploration missions.

Find Out Even More

Using search engines like Google or Bing to find information about subjects you love, you'll find millions of results. Searching for "European Space Agency (ESA)," leads to millions of sites. There are around 10 million results if you're using Google!

When you search for European Space Agency (ESA), you'll get many different kinds of search results. Some of them are good. Many of them will be great sources of information about deep space exploration. Others, however, are not so good. They won't be results you'll want to click on or sites you want to visit when looking for facts about space probes.

ESA
www.esa.int

European Space Agency - Wikipedia, the free encyclopedia
en.wikipedia.org/wiki/European_Space_Agency

ESA - YouTube
www.youtube.com/user/ESA

ESA (esa) on Twitter
twitter.com/esa

NASA/ESA Hubble Space Telescope
www.spacetelescope.org

And these are just a few results from the first page! There are millions more. The ESA has many sites. They have a Twitter page and a YouTube page. These are official pages on sites like Facebook and Twitter that allow people to follow the ESA. They are good sources of information, but you can get more information reading sites like www. spacetelescope.org.

Wikipedia can be a great place to learn a few quick facts. But don't forget to check for the small numbers near the facts you read on Wikipedia. Clicking these numbers takes you to the source of the information on Wikipedia. Not every fact on Wikipedia is true. Checking the source of the information is the best way to make sure a fact is true. Official sources like www.esa.int or www.nasa.gov are better sources.

Not all search results are the same. And not all key words are the same. Search for "ESA," and you can get sites like these:

The Entertainment Software Association - Home Page
www.theesa.com

Home | Entomological Society of America (ESA)
www.entsoc.org

Eastern Surfing Association: the best amateur surfing organization ...
www.surfesa.org

Searching for almost any subject will get you millions of results. You can never see them all, but you'll always have something new to check out on the Internet!

FOUR

What Comes Next?

W e know there is a lot of deep space out there. So far, we've only explored a tiny part of it. But as the years go on, we'll learn more and more about the rest of the universe.

Going and Going

Don't forget, the *Voyager* missions are still out there. They have passed by Jupiter, Saturn, Uranus, and Neptune. Now they are continuing on out of the solar system.

Voyager 2 still has a long way to go before it leaves the solar system. But scientists argue whether or not *Voyager 1* has already made the leap. *Voyager 1* has definitely traveled a very long way. Some people are convinced it has traveled so far that is has made it beyond the solar

system. Other people argue the opposite. Scientists can tell that Sun has a lot less influence wherever *Voyager 1* is now, but the effects of the Sun are still there.

Once the mission leaves the Sun's magnetic field, it will really be outside the solar system. Scientists aren't exactly sure when that will happen. They don't know how big the solar system is. The *Voyager* missions are the first time we've sent any spacecraft so far. Even if it hasn't left the solar system yet, *Voyager*'s mission is still pretty amazing.

Technology is something humans invent to make something easier or go somewhere new.

New Horizons

Even with new *technology*, spacecraft need a long time to get to objects out in deep space. That's true of the *New Horizons* mission to Pluto.

Scientists have debated whether or not Pluto is a planet for many years. Today they classify it as a dwarf planet. Whatever it is, it's still an interesting space object to study!

NASA launched the *New Horizons* spacecraft in 2006. The spacecraft had to travel 3 billion miles (5 billion kilometers or 32 astronomical units) to get to its destination! So far *New Horizons* has passed by Mars, Jupiter, Saturn, and Uranus. It is set to get to Pluto by 2015.

This mission will be the first to really study Pluto. Scientists want to know what Pluto's atmosphere is made out of. They want to know what the surface looks like. All the instruments on board *New Horizons* will give them that information.

Better Technology

Space exploration technology has gotten a lot better since we started launching things into space in the 1950s. Technology has gotten us to the moon, Mars, Jupiter, Saturn, and beyond. And technology can take us even farther with more success! NASA recently picked three new projects to work on to make deep-space exploration better. NASA chose a deep-space atomic clock, a solar-powered sail, and a way of communicating with lasers. The atomic clock will make missions run more precisely. The sail will help missions fly faster. And the lasers will let far-away spacecraft send data back to Earth really fast. One space mission that uses each technology will be launched in a few years.

The New Horizons *spacecraft shown above is on its way to Pluto. It will give us a closer look at what it's like so far out from the sun.*

Planet or Not?

After Pluto was discovered in 1930, everyone called it a planet. People considered it the ninth planet in the solar system, out beyond Neptune. Then astronomers made more space discoveries. They discovered the Kuiper Belt, an area in space beyond Neptune that has many, many space objects. Maybe Pluto was just one of the bigger objects in the Kuiper Belt and not a planet after all. The International Astronomical Union met in 2006 to decide whether Pluto was a planet or not. This is the organization that decides on things like the names of space objects. It decided that planets have to orbit the Sun. They have to be round. And they have to have enough gravity to attract other space objects like moons to them. The Union decided Pluto didn't fit that definition. Other scientists disagreed and were angry, but the decision was made.

The parts on the spacecraft will start to wear down during such a long trip. *New Horizons* has two of most parts. If one fails, the other one will hopefully work.

Who knows what's next for space exploration? NASA has proposed missions to Uranus. We don't know much about that planet. More missions would help us learn a lot more.

A Uranus mission won't happen for a while. NASA is focusing on Mars. NASA also wants to study asteroids more closely. And NASA doesn't have a lot of money for as much space exploration as in the past.

But a trip to the farthest planets in the solar system could happen in the future. So could more journeys outside the solar system. Deep space is big! There's a lot to explore—and a lot to learn!

Find Out Even More

Every site is different. Some sites have better information than other sites. Some sites aren't about facts at all. Blogs and social media sites like Facebook or Twitter aren't always good sources of information about space exploration. Knowing what you're reading and who wrote is an important part of searching for information online. Each person has a different point of view. On the Internet, each website is made by different people. And people make websites for many different reasons.

Not everyone posts good information and everyone has their own rules about what can be posted and what cannot. A website like www.nasa.gov is a good source of information, but this is not true of every site. Just because you read something on the Internet, that doesn't always mean it's true.

When you're searching for information on the Internet, ask yourself a few questions about the sites you visit:

1. Who made the site? Why did they make the site? Knowing who made the site and why they made it is a good way of deciding if it has good information. On www.nasa.gov, you can see the NASA logo in the corner. You know the site was made by NASA, so you know it's a good source of information about space exploration.
2. Do you think the site you're using a good source of information?

3. How is the site organized? Can you search for topics that you want to learn more about? Can you choose different categories or pages on the site to help you find what you're looking for?
4. How old is the information on the site? Can you find a date on the article or post? Can you find another site with more up-to-date information? Try adding "news" to the key words you're using in search engines to find the latest facts.
5. What do you like about the site? What would you change about the site? Why? Would you use the site again? Just as books are each different, each site is different. Finding sites you like makes finding new information and learning new things fun.

Remember to ask yourself these questions about the sites you visit, and you'll be on your way to figuring out which sites are good and which aren't. Sorting good information from bad information is a big part of learning online. You've got to be the judge of the sites you visit!

Here's What We Recommend

If you want to learn more about deep-space probes and space exploration, here are some good websites and books to get you started!

Online

KidsAstronomy.com: Deep Space
www.kidsastronomy.com/deep_space.htm

NASA Kids' Club
www.nasa.gov/audience/forkids/kidsclub/flash/index.html

National Geographic: Space Exploration
science.nationalgeographic.com/science/space/space-exploration

Space.com
www.space.com

In Books

Dugan, Christine. *Space Exploration (Time for Kids)*. Huntington Beach, Calif.: Teacher Created Materials, 2012.

Goldsmith, Mike. *Universe: Journey into Deep Space*. New York: Kingfisher, 2012.

Miller, Ron. *Space Exploration*. Minneapolis, Minn.: Twenty-First Century Books, 2008.

Stott, Carole. *Space Exploration*. New York: DK Publishing, 2009.

Index

About the Author

Kim Etingoff lives in Boston, Massachusetts, spending part of her time working on farms. Kim writes educational books for young people on topics including health, science, history, and more.

Picture Credits

www.ingramcontent.com/pod-product-compliance
Lightning Source LLC
Chambersburg PA
CBHW040749100426
42735CB00034B/94